Agnes Török is an award-winr
TED speaker and author. Thei
and activism.

Török has produced poetry in
organisations and campaigns f
cultural institutions such as Rou .... aııu ıne BBC.

Török has toured on four continents and written books in two
languages about mental health, gender-based violence, the rise
of the extreme right, and feminist and queer resistance.

Török lives in Stockholm, Sweden, with their communities and
pot plants. Their supporters live around the world.

All the Days We Don't Revolt is Agnes' fifth book, and the one
closest to their hopelessly optimistic heart.

all the days we don't revolt

AGNES TÖRÖK

Burning Eye

Burning Eye Books
Never Knowingly
Mainstream

This edition published by Burning Eye Books 2020

www.burningeye.co.uk
@burningeyebooks

Burning Eye Books
15 West Hill, Portishead, BS20 6LG

ISBN 978-1-911570-71-4

all the days we don't revolt

contents

we love & learn

we revolt anyway

bonus: writing revolts

outro: how we revolt every day

intro:

what do we do

on all the days we don't

revolt?

For a long time, I have felt the tension of trying to change the world – and live in it while I do.

Not surprising with the state of the world. And not something I believe I am alone in feeling.

That sense of guilt at missing a family member's birthday party to go to a protest. Or, worse yet, missing a protest to go to a birthday party. Even your own. Or is one really better or worse than the other? Aren't they both part of sustaining the good things and changing the things that are everything but?

For me, there has been a sense of not doing enough to make the world a better place. Not working hard enough against systems of oppression. Not compensating enough for the state the world's in. Not mobilising enough of my time or ability to build something better.

I think there is a point to this restlessness, this sense of discomfort with allowing things to remain the way they are. There is great purpose to holding ourselves and each other accountable. To wanting to make the world better.

But I also know that this guilt of 'never enough' is dangerous and counter-productive. That some of the most brilliant activists and change-makers I know have been burnt out and driven to exhaustion by 'never enough'.

That there needs to be some living to balance out the revolting. That we need to be able to change the world and eat our birthday cake too.

We nurture & nourish

'Burned out activists can't change the world, and trying to do everything yourself will make any campaign fall apart.

   If you want to change the world, first, look after yourselves, and then look after your comrades, and then work together to look after your movement.'

Harry Josephine Giles

all the living

I want to write a poem
      about all the poems I don't write

all the things I don't consider important enough
to be turned into
      manifestos

        like planting flowers in the spring

      patience and work and watching things grow
    nurturing and creating and letting life unfold
time and love and hope and care

there's just not much of a rallying cry there

    not much of a slogan
    not much of a banner
    a hashtag / protest chant / struggle song

I want to write a poem
    about all the poems I don't write

I want to write a book
    about all the days we don't revolt

all the stillness / the quiet / the ordinary
    that keeps us going

all the little sunlight glimpses of daily life
that give us the strength
to carry on revolting

all the meals
    people have cooked to take care of me
all the sofas
    someone's offered me to crash on
all the hugs

I have been given
    after meetings
    after trials
    after political victories
after elections
after disappointing news
after me and us and you

all the loving we've done
    all the falling apart
        and putting back together again
        all the letters
        all the calls
        all the cups of tea

the movies we've watched in silence
when we no longer have words
to put the hardness of the world into

when we collapse into familiarities
put together jigsaw puzzles
listen to audiobooks
go for walks
just to do
something
        other than
giving up

all the flowers we've planted
the sheets we've washed
the birthday presents
the farewell parties
the 'are you OK's

    all the living we did
      that gave us the strength

        to keep revolting

because it has to be true

that there are
enough
good people

in this world

to make the
world
good
too

just pores and feelings

all my friends are

brain heart sorrow laughter love comfort hope

they struggle and try again
place two feet
on the cold floor beside the bed each morning and find some way
    any way
        to get up

they look out of the hollows
of their own stress tiredness heartache
    and find a way to reach into mine

    friendship is a conversation
    it's existing in relation
    letting others form part of you

    allowing yourself to be changed by others loving you

        inviting people to get so close
        that you're not impressive anymore

you're just pores and feelings

just gunk between your teeth
and trying to make sense of it all

just sleep in your eyes
and drool on your cheek

    and being there for each other anyway
        loving anyway

        there are days
        I find protest
        and even poetry
        pointless

but
        never
                you

                        I find you
                        and I know
                        I can stop searching

what keeps me going

every last one of you
who have picked me up
when I have fallen

    told me I am enough
    when I feel paper-thin

      reminded me I am not alone
  in needing to believe
that a good life is possible

        even while
          we are fighting
            for a better
             world

i take myself out

for coffee for walks for adventures
to the cinema the beach the library

      we go on little dates
      me and myself

            try to remind ourself
            that life shouldn't be
            work-until-you-hit-the-wall
            that it can't be all tour or all Netflix

I go on trips with friends
to where they live to where I live
to the forest the mountains
the place we learn something

or else a café where we can chat until we do

      we travel together
      me and my chosen family
      build and strengthen that which bends
      and breaks too quickly

      we give ourselves time
            to do all the catching up

            to see what happens after
      when nothing is on our minds
and we are perfectly in sync

      to see what is spoken
      in the silence

            what we learn about joy
            when we are not so busy

            chasing it

hope

revolt in your daily life

by finding joy against all odds
by refusing to value yourself the way the market does
by being kind to people even when it gives you nothing

> except your humanity

revolt by cooking by eating by sleeping by fucking by loving
by friending by attending
> revolt by speaking out by knowing when to shut up
> > by listening
> > > by being attentive
> > > by learning how to stand in solidarity with others
> > how to sing songs because others need the silence filled
how to quiet down because others need the space to speak

revolt by making by co-creating by overthrowing the myth of the
individual by being part of something greater by becoming
bigger than the sum of your parts by caring for others

revolt by planting
by nurturing
by believing that no matter how bleak things look
there will again come a spring
and when it does
you will be there to meet it
> > > face facing the sun

revolt by recognising that hope is our most precious resource
that when it runs out everything else feels empty
that there are political projects based on us being so worried
about the immediate present that we never lift our gaze and think
about where we want to be heading together

to resist means to be able to step back
and think about the bigger picture

to resist we must sustain hope
we must find the seeds of it and
grow it nurture it harvest it redistribute it

      revolt by recognising that some days we will fail
          to be the kinds of revolutionaries
            we would like to be
              (and that's OK)

          that self-compassion is also kindness
        that kindness is also revolt
      that self-care is part of community care
but not the entirety of it

revolt by allowing others to shift priorities
even when you would like them to be focused
on what you think is most important

      because life happens
      (let it)

revolt by allowing yourself to love too
to care too
to be hurt too

revolt by allowing your full humanity
     and recognising
        always
           that humanity in others

      revolt by refusing to give in
         by crashing into open arms
           by bunking down and holding on
              when nothing else feels possible

but never

never ever

giving up

on

hope

i learnt this from my grandmother

it's one of those days
my partner comes home
from the news of
yet another deportation
just as I'm getting ready
for a funeral

      we kiss
      cook
      eat

don't know what else to do

her shirt says *QUEER SOLIDARITY SMASHES BORDERS*
      her eyes say she's struggling to believe it today

      my funeral dress
      looks serious
      does not feel like me
      I put an apron over it

when even poets
run out of words
            we turn to action
            repeated a thousand times
            it becomes ritual
            healing
            holy

            ginger, garlic and chili in the pan
I learnt this from my mother
cooking your way through heartache

      I fry the vegetables
      she marinates the tofu

'they're deporting him to his death
they know that'

silence
there is nothing to say

this is the way
we have always done it

falling apart
and putting ourselves
back together again

'the ceremony was beautiful
but it doesn't make them less dead'

I cook the noodles
she adds the soy

I learnt this from my grandmother
on her way from cancer surgery
she calls me

'we have to be optimistic'
she says
'or what else do we have?'

so we cook

nurture

what we can

i go to museums

to get inspired
to remind myself that humans in all our chaos
      can create as well as destroy

I go to museums
to wander around
      convince myself
      that the world is OK
              or else could be

but it doesn't work

the museums are filled with history
a vase
      next to jewels stolen under colonialism
a bust
      beside a painting of a road that cost 10,000
      enslaved lives to build

beside the modernists are the Nazis
beside the romantics are their nationalist wars

      in front of it all
      rows upon rows
      of schoolchildren

          learning about
          The Glorious Past

I go to museums
but not to be inspired
      not anymore

          I go to get angry

          and to make something better

             in place of the past

rain dogs

there is rain against the window

a great book in my hand

and I have someone to long for

      I wonder
           if this isn't the most
                 quietly magical
                     feeling there is

something old, something new

family
is my mum calling

to ask if I'll give her grown-up points
for cleaning her flat

      she is fifty-three
      I give her the points

      family
      is birthday parties / getting fired / break-
      ups / celebrations / new jobs

          moving away
     and moving back
and someone helping you carry the heavy load

      first days of term
      and last goodbyes in hospitals
      and all the days in between

family
is my best friend knowing me so well
      for so long
          that we joke that her memory
              is my external hard drive

'you haven't worn a striped shirt since fifth grade'
she tells me when we meet for coffee
'I haven't?' I ask
'no. still suits you, though'

      family
      is siblings and parents and cousins
      turning up at your door
          in a different country
      because you don't have to say it
      for them to notice
          you're needing help to cope

family
is chosen
        is the friendships that have lasted so long
        outlived so many romantic relationships
you've started celebrating your anniversaries BIG

for your first friendiversary
        you go to Amsterdam
        get drunk and plan the next ten years

for your eighth friendiversary
        you climb a mountain
        ride the Hogwarts train
        both admit you still believe in magic

for your group friendiversary
        you wade across a national park
        in frozen water
        get lost on a road trip
        because all four of you
        needed to see a medieval castle

for the full decade
        you take your assess
                all the way to Disneyland
                because what the hell
        you never had a chance to do it
        when you were kids

        and you are still just as excited about
        talking animals and spaceships
        princesses and rainbows
                as you were back then

family
is the people you choose
and the people who choose you

        is twelve separate people calling
        just to see how you're doing
        when you've told just one
        you're having a hard time

30

it's having someone
who would always be happy
to hear from you

it's knowing that with some people
you are always on call

family
is alternative Christmas
we celebrate after the real one

for friends whose families
won't accept them, their names or their pronouns
it's choosing to be family for one another

it's emergency rooms
and bubbly stuff in glasses
leftover fridge food
and childhood balloons

family
is the choice to care for one another
every single day

family
is my mum calling
to ask if I'll give her grown-up points
for working really hard this week

I say
'if I can have points too'

she's fifty-three
I'm twenty-six

we both deserve the points

slow

I've been
stressing running doing projecting
    just to get back to you each night
        and kiss the tired away

I've been
planning budgeting overviewing communicating
and seeing friends and family
has started to feel
just like

meetings

        except we hug at the end

I've been
hoping feeling thinking dreaming
about a time when it's not like this
when I've got
space
to
breathe

    but the horizon
    doesn't get any closer
    no matter how fast I run

so now I'm

        sitting
      giving myself time to rest
    learning to take on the role of student
    acknowledging I don't know
    how to do   everything
    especially not at once
    especially not at alone

learning

step by step

how to live

slow

all the days we don't revolt

activism isn't a lifestyle
                        it can't be
                        not for most people
and not for long

I've seen the best minds of my generation
                    lost to burn-out
                    to all-or-nothing politics

                                to the choice between
total self-serving
                        or
                                total self-sacrifice

                as if we didn't need
                sustainability
                in our environmental movements

        as if we didn't need to
        pay rent
        while we campaign for better housing

as if we didn't need to share
the emotional labour
of carrying our feminist /
anti-racist /
queer /
crip /

class-conscious
progressive movements

when we talk about who is expected
to do what
and who gets the credit for it

as if we could ever
afford to
forget

that we have to find ways
to live in the world
while we are
changing it

we build communities

'I want another way of relating where we are doing reciprocal care work for each other, one where we are figuring out more kind and interdependent ways of coexisting, recognising that mental and physical wellness aren't individual shortcomings but rather collective concerns.'

Alok Vaid-Menon

the simplest thing

I've been trying to write a million poems
just to tell you the simplest thing:

     if you feel hopeless
     you are not alone

        if you choose
        to act anyway

            there are
            a thousands
            open arms

                right here

        waiting

   to welcome you

while we waited for the revolution

while we waited for the revolution
    we planted sunflower seeds
        in tin cans
        stole the soil
        and lent the sunshine

                watched something hopeful grow

while we waited for the revolution
    we went to marches
    signed petitions
    organised resistances
wrote and spoke and listened

while we waited for the revolution
    we drank wine in flats
    we could barely afford
    complained about dead-end jobs
    made meals for friends down on their luck
waited for the other shoe to drop

while we waited for the revolution
    we argued about how best to go about it
    passionately joined
    and were quickly disillusioned with
political parties and progressive organisations
banners and hashtags and movements for change

    we went on campaign trails
    collected donations
    took arduous stands

        stumbled and fell
      exhausted or elated
    celebrating or disappointed
      alone or together
        into bed

and in sleep
we dreamt of tomorrows
where we weren't waiting anymore

in the mornings
we woke up
and tried again

protest

our bodies
moving together

      sacred

our lungs
singing together

      temple

our feet
marching together

      ancient

our hope
building together

      movement

superheroes

we're superheroes
only no one can tell

      instead of capes and Spandex
      we wear coffee stains
      and bags under our eyes

but we're superheroes
      you can see it
            if you look close enough

look at the way she is texting on the bus
checking in with her friend
who hasn't got out of bed
since the last horrid news cycle

      look at the way they have paint stains
      on their fingers
      distractedly pick it off on the morning bus
      tired from being up all night
      painting the signs for tomorrow's protest

      look at the way the flour's spread
      all over his jeans
      how he wipes his hands on them
      waiting at the traffic light
      on his way to the bake sale fundraiser

look at the way they sit at that library table
all those teens the adults think
only care about their phones
look at them   totally quiet

typing / posting / hashtagging an online uprising into being
raising awareness to keep the hospital / library / women's aid /
community centre / school
from being shut down

look closely
notice their superpower

solidarity
made verb

empathy
turned into action

something/anything/more

sometimes we've just gotta do something even when we know it's not enough to change everything because doing nothing feels like giving up and that's the one thing we can't afford because doing something anything is how we build the stamina to do

more

burn, they said

all my friends are fighting the good fight
all my friends have burnt out

all my friends are gender-dysphoric post-traumatic anxious
depressed
       and still out marching for a tomorrow
       that looks a bit less shit than this

all my friends were told they could be anything
       and we wanted to be the revolution

       we were told we should be the change
       we wanted to see in the world
       and we tried to be   perfect

           we were told to go out
      and make our dreams come true
      to pull ourselves up by the bootstraps
to be the best we could be
to go. all. out.

and all my friends have burnt out

we grew up on a steady diet
of social media and no food

      gotta get that thigh gap
      while we fight the wage gap

the revolution will not be televised
but we're just gonna post this march real quick
to make sure more people come to it

      we're just gonna explain sexism to you
        racism to you
        transphobia to you
        homophobia to you

ableism classism ageism to you

as if you couldn't Google that shit

we'll do the laundry and the heavy lifting
carry the care and the coping mechanisms

we do the paid work and the unpaid work
and when all that's done
of course we'll listen to your problems, hon!
we'll do the emotional labour too
'cause what the hell
that's what femmes and queers
are supposed to do

and none of my friends can get out of bed
and half of them have gone ill with the stress
and we're just trying to do our best

only it's not good enough
never good enough

and we missed another hashtag
march and petition
another day at work
another class

and the world's moving so fast
the world's moving so quickly now
was it always moving this quickly?
were we always juggling this much?

around the clock and every day
our phones are ticking time bombs
they can go off at any time

we get emails at midnight with the title URGENT
we get work calls on all our days off
an online storm will come at us in the middle of our week of

vacation
      I mean workcation
            when we catch up on all the shit
                 we never have time to do

                    while we work
                        for pay

and we are too tired to keep marching

and we are too stressed to resist and shout

and we are too exhausted from carrying it all

          and all my friends

                  have burnt out

the way the world is fucked

I am learning how to be kind to myself
    to recognise that
        the way the world is fucked
        is not due to my personal failures

        that I am part of a species
        whose job it is to fix it
        all the same

           this difference
      not my personal fault
    but our collective responsibility

means that I can do the task joyfully
with the skills and experiences at my disposal

    without expecting myself or others
      to know the whole plan
        alone

it's been said

it's been said
no one has the patience for movements anymore

people join for a hashtag / a petition / a protest
but they don't stick around for the careful work
of long-term societal change

it's been said
no one has the energy for friendships anymore

    people swipe / flirt / date
    and when it gets difficult
no one's willing to work it out
for long enough to make a friendship in its place

        nothing wrong with that
        looking for the easy way
            nothing wrong with that
            wanting the instantaneous
        but it's not how we build change
    it's not how we build care
it's not how we make things sustainable
these things we'd love to make
    like love and revolution

it's been said
we don't have the attention span for it

that my generation's been raised on social media notifications
and fast food fundraising fury
    that we don't have what it takes
    to stick around and embed change
    deep within the layers of our societies

it's been said
            and I think they're wrong about us
                    us millennials / gen Zs
                    youngsters / kids these days

it's been said
and I want to say it differently

                        that our best
            and most revolutionary days
                            are still ahead of us

(un)learning

changing anything starts with understanding
what you thought you knew to be obvious
needs to be re-examined and reconsidered

    unlearning the idea that
    the way things are is the way things
    have always and will always be

        if we are to make any change
        we need to learn to be OK
            with being uncomfortable

        allyship isn't about your comfort
    but about assisting where you're needed
in making the world a better place

the reward is in the world
you are part of building

so don't expect a pat on your back

if you are committing to change
for other people's validation
you will become bitter and entitled

    if as a male feminist
    if as a white anti-racist
    if as a cis, straight person at Pride

        if as a person with privilege
    you expect those who are oppressed
to be grateful to you for helping

you. are. not. helping.

    your ego is in the front seat
the movement is only a vehicle for you
and it will not take you where you want to go

but if you are willing to learn
to sit quietly and cringe at your past self
when you see the world in a new light

if you're willing to lend hands and heart
when and where they are needed
then we're on to something

it's good to recognise
that you have done wrong in the past
it means you are doing better now

when someone with lived experience
challenges your point
or problematises your privilege

they are handing you a gift
offering you an opportunity to learn
giving of their time and experience

and you owe it
to the movement
to consider their point

because creating change
means learning
and unlearning

you do not need to be perfect
you just need to be willing
to be better than you were

the one who comes through

I am so used to being
the out-of-town success story
        to showing up and dazzling out
                leaving as everyone's favourite

without having to do any of the work

how many birthdays have I missed
while I've been out
travelling studying working careering campaigning revolting?

how many hospital visit hand-holdings
        were I not around for?

        it is easy to be the one that comes and goes
        the one with all the families and lovers
                greeted at any airport
                any train station
            by someone who is
            genuinely happy to see you

I've become so used to leaving
to stretching my affections to breaking point
across oceans and patchy connections

        the terrifying loss of hope
        of at least one of the countries I call home
        at any point in time

I am so used to leaving
        that at first I didn't recognise this feeling
                this weight like tired
        this fear like abandonment
this sense of being the one who gets left behind

                because now I am the one staying
        the one holding space
planning life around others' arrival dates

the one making room
the one making it work
the one doing the work
of loving

I am so used to leaving
to the particular pain of departures
I forgot how much it hurts
to be the one who stays

and there is silver lining to this hurt
it is called loving

and there is intertwining to this hurt
it is called caring

and there is fortifying to this hurt
and it is called returning to each other
and ourselves

all those phone calls
all those messages letters flowers
birthday presents 'are you OK's

all the work of staying close
when one of you can't stay

I got used to being
the glimmer
the blossoming
the spring

I am learning to be the one
who sticks around
when things get difficult
cold, dark and blue

learning how to be the one

who comes through

may day

gathered like this
we feel powerful
hopeful
right

        like we have a magical ability
            and it is to come together
                to fight
                    for better

like I have a secret power
    and it's my words
    my weapon / my armour

    I want to find a way
    to harvest this feeling
    to crystallise and bottle it
    for rainy days
    we know are coming

we do not fight off fascism in a day
we do not reverse climate change overnight
we do not win against the extreme right

                by marching
                together
                alone

but this is how we gather the strength
to keep going

    when keeping going
    feels damn near pointless

      I want to savour it
      this one victory

    I want to celebrate it
    this giant step in the right direction

I want to believe it to be true
what feels so obvious today

that what they call
inevitable

we can change

dance

I want it to feel like a dance
 the way we move together in crowds

I want it to feel like a song
 the way we sing together for change

I want it to feel like a long-lost kiss
 the way we talk about the future we miss

I want it to be

art we make collaboratively

the way we come together

to build a different world

we care & create

'Art must peddle hope to a cynical world.'

Rupi Kaur

something like optimism

not knowing how to do it

but genuinely believing

we'll work it out

the right amount of revolution

I wish I could tell you
how to set the world right

wish I had an answer
        to all your questions

                or half of mine

            wish I had
        a step-by-step plan
a ten-point to-do list of how to change it all

                                    I don't

                        what I have
                    are words

                what I know
            is the relationship
        between me and the page
between the page and the world

                sometimes I think
        that's all I'm capable of

    and maybe
            just maybe
                    that's enough

writer wife

our friendship
    is vulnerability
        companionship
            taking care of each other
      helping one another
   feel OK about taking care
of ourselves

it's this pain in my chest when we say goodbye
        and I don't know when I'll see you again

the fact that I have a pen tattooed on my arm
    but you're the one I trust
      with my writing

    (thank you for helping me edit this book)

    it's messages and letters and 'are you OK's

trusting each other's
creative processes so much
that we decide on a whim
    to write a book together
     and then actually do it

it's coffee in the sun in your country
and tea in the snow in mine

    it's all the years
    we help each other power through

      all the ways
      we empower and encourage
      one another

        to write

        our own

        revolutions

art is empathy

maybe the reason
we are so interested
     in the extremes of human experience

     the fantastic and the ordinary

          maybe the reason
          we are so interested
          in fictional stories

     is not because they differ
     from reality

but because we hope
they will change it

poem in the making

there are poems
        that turn me on
                and leave me wanting more

there are poems that open the door
        and say 'here
                step into yourself
                        make yourself at home'

there are poems that remind you
        of what's important
                that make you feel alive
                        in ways you'd forgotten
                                that you could

        poems that fill you up with 'I will'
                        instead of 'I should'

                there are poems
      in the
                              silence
      between the beats

so ecstatic
      you'll be screaming them out

      there's a poem
      for everyone

          there's a poem
          for every moment

there's a poem happening

      right here

right now

someone really ought to write it down

committed reader

I am an avid reader
keep a book with me at all times
but I am not a committed one
 I fall out of books howling
 like an abandoned lover
  looking for a rebound

 half-opened quarter-read books
 litter my nightstand
nothing catches my attention for long

 I think maybe I can manage casual
date a book with a pretty cover and a few laughs

 I almost always give up halfway through

what was meant to be a way to fill my evenings
manages to not keep me busy until I fall asleep

what is it with all these one-night-stand stories?
these books that crumble in on themselves
the second you start wondering what they're for

 a few times in my life
 I have found grand romance in a book
 sheltered myself away for days
 pillow-talking my way through the nights
 with stories that manage to keep me up
  no matter how tired I am

in the mornings I've thought of the characters
 before I've really woken
  and it's a joy to see it there
 the open chapter smiling back at me
like sunlight in my eyes

  there are loves I return to
 covers I have fingered into unreadability
 pages I know so intimately

I no longer need to read them
I know them off by heart

these are friends now
lovers that stay with you for life

and so when I pick that book up at the library
        sure, I've got hope
                sure, I have heard great things
but will it still be there in the morning
        or will I have given up
                any hope of longevity
                        before it even began?

I am an avid reader
keep a book with me at all times
        but I am not a committed one
        a book needs to earn my attention
                for me to stick around

        so when I find a book that has it all
        politics and poetry and adventure

when a book tells me something about myself
I'd not put into words before
when a book shows me the horizon
inside my own bedroom door

                when a book earns my reading
        trust me
I am never putting it down
        again

writing heartbreak

if there is any comfort to being a poet
it is this:

> just as I feel I am losing you
> I get to turn us into poetry

if there is any comfort to being a poet
it is this:

> all these little failures
>   all these loves-that-did-not-become

>   instead become art

>   made meaningful

> by its making

fuck potential

fuck potential
screw everything we might be
                         could be
                 will one day become

fuck talent
        inborn inbred bloody skill
                as if we didn't have to earn it all
            work and sweat and bleed it bead it
each droplet forming and falling from us
blood, sweat and tears

as if all that becoming
            was something
                    that happened without us

as if spring
            didn't have to work twice as hard
                                as fall

as if it isn't easier to let things crumble
than to dare to build something new

            never knowing if it will work
            never knowing where you'll end up
                or how you'll get here

            if you can make any of it come true
                    never knowing if dreams
                    were meant for someone like you

fuck potential
we make it ourselves
        mix it into breakfast
        drink it down as pints
                stir it in our innards
                    when we
            work practise rehearse
        try and try again

71

when we dare to fail
fail again
fail better

when we dare to say
no and fuck no
and I would do anything for my big break
but I won't do that

when we dare to have morals
and hold integrity
dare to rest
and set boundaries
when we build different
set our own goals and frames of reference
our own judges, co-creators and conspirators

when we pull our roots from the earth
and say
no pasarán
we are not moving
not one step further
we are not there yet
but we will be
I believe it
we will be

like a hymn sung by a thousand atheists

call it work call it pragmatism
call it the school of life
call it whatever you fucking want

fuck potential
we are living now

making now

changing now

we will not wait until you validate it

we are not here to get hired or to get paid
we are here to live and make and change
try and create and revolt
        every single day

so fuck potential
    we're not waiting anymore

worry & stress

I am great at both
     and have learned the hard way

     worry is just stress

     without a deadline

artsy cis men

I'm just writing my work
I'm just living my truth
I'm just keeping my typing fingers down
                           my head up
                                 and my tongue in place

I'm just biding my time
I'm just building my platforms
I'm just getting ready for a fight
                you haven't even realised is coming

        and artsy cis men ask me
                where did all this success come from?
                what are your connections?
        meaning
                who did you sleep with to get to where you are?

                        and I tell them
                I'm just doing the work
        instead of talking about it

I'm just taking a stand
instead of dancing around the problem

I'm just learning the craft
instead of faking it (and asking someone else to cover my ass)

        all you're doing is having that extra beer
        at the pub after the gig
                for networking
                you say

while I wake up at 6am
        sit down in front of my laptop
                and do the fucking work

while you're sleeping off your hangover
I've written three poems before breakfast every day for years

while you're sharing photos
of the crazy party after the gig last night
I've written another book
without anyone asking me to or giving me a deadline

because I don't do the work to get credit
because I don't do the work to get laid
because I don't do the work to get famous or drunk or rich

I do the work because I believe in the work
I write the words because I know what I want to say
and who I want to say it to

I do the work
because it is part of actively changing the world
and to do that work we need to be strategic
and we need to work our asses off

so I edit and publish and plan and market and network and
collaborate and do the lights at the gig and do the sound at
the gig and do the accounting after the gig and respond to the
emails and send the thank-yous and donate the proceeds to
charity and plan for the next gig

all in the time it takes you to post about
how cool you look on stage

so, artsy cis men
who are not willing to do the work
who are not willing to learn the work
to respect the work
to put the time in
to put the effort in
to do it all for the chance it gives you
to speak about what really matters

so, artsy cis men
who have nothing to say
about what really matters
but want to be in the spotlight when they say it

know that there are legions of femmes and queers just like me

        and we are just biding our time
     and we are just holding our tongues
  and we are just doing the work

   and soon

   you won't know
   what hit you

my mother's shirt

months ago
I started writing
in my mother's old shirt
    I guess it makes me feel safe

     like when the words
     lead me to the ledge of myself
     and say 'jump'
   it's an anchor
to pull me back in again

    like when the poem
    has me not just under pressure
       but opening the floodgates
       and letting it all out

           it might not show
       but there's blood on this page
       there's ache in this words
     and you can't tell
     but I cried while writing this

    writing is the most honest thing I do
the most courageous
the thing that brings me out of everything called safety
      and still leads me back home
   hand in hand
shows me the bed

     says
        come rest here
I have made you a pillow
      out of words
        it is soft

      and it will let you sleep
        without nightmares

and maybe
      when you wake again
      the world
      will be a better place

bricks

I write because it makes me human

    I write because some days I wake up
        and it's all I can do not to fall apart again

I write because I hope I can write us a place free from all this

    that with words I can build town squares
    and with verbs I can build parks
        and with metaphors I can make people meet
    and with similes I can make smiles spread
as eyes connect

that with a whisper of my voice or a stroke of my pen
I can build us a place

where we can imagine a future different from this
where we can sit and talk and think and feel
    and find a way to make it all real

and when I don't see a way to do it with mortar and brick
    with closed mouth and raised fists
        I turn to words
        and I think
            maybe
        just maybe

    this is how we build it

    a vision of a future together

we love & learn

'We work too hard.
We're too tired
to fall in love.

Therefore we must
overthrow the government.'

Rod Smith

love in the time of the alt-right

is it wrong, me sitting here
writing love poems
when the world is going to shit?

what could be more important
than loving you
when the world looks like this?

i'll take this one

'I'll take this one and you get the next, yeah?'

I love being surrounded by femmes and queers
because we're not dividing rounds of pints at the pub
we're rotating who does the work and who gets to rest
      put their feet up
           have a cup of tea
                take the pressure off

'I'll take this one and you get the next, yeah?'

I'll do this bit of cooking / cleaning / admin / child care / marching
hospital visit / meeting with the immigration office
birthday party planning / nappy-changing / calling the tax office
crying / hosting / emotional labour
            and I know you'll do the next

                        because that's how it goes with us
                  because that's how we've built
        our communities

my hands become your hands become ours

        here is the work that needs doing
our mouths say
        here are the hands to do it

we are resources for collective resistance

        I offer my hands and you take them in yours
            look me in the eye
            tell me to sit down and put my feet up for a bit

'I'll take this one and you get the next, yeah?'

'yes, please. thank you'

how could i regret loving them?

it taught me
everything I know
     about resilience

     about what I am
        willing
            to put up with

               and how capable I am
               of fighting against
               what I will not

a homage. a love letter. a recipe

this is a homage
to nappy changes and nightmare saves
to breakfast follies and bedtime stories
to mittens found and lost and found again
to hugs lasting however long or short I wanted

to breakfasts and lunches and snacks and dinners
and dishes and dishes and dishes
and laundry and laundry and laundry

to packed bags on Mondays
moving this way and that

to all the things you did to raise me
to all the love I never went without

this is a love letter
to the handiwork of parenting
the act of family
the verb of safety

you made this   everything I stand on
you made this   everything I've become
you made this   every joy that's come to be

you made this
everything I am

you made me

reclaim love

maybe
      just maybe

            it's possible to reclaim

                  everything I gave up

                        to survive

loving again

it's like all those stories you hear as a kid
the chorus of every sappy song you've dismissed
those long-forgotten hopes you've hidden within yourself
    all coming true

        loving again
        after leaving abuse

          and you realise
          you're capable of loving

            and you realise
          you are capable of building love
       with someone who doesn't harm you
    someone who doesn't see you as a function
but a person

      and you realise
      how much loss there is
         to this
           losing your value
              in the eyes of someone you love

and you realise
it's day one again
      and you are brand new in this world
      and love is just as scary and just as big
           just as balloon-in-the-chest wonderful
           as it was when you were a teenager

              and the world was at your feet

and there's this rhythm that's been playing inside you
for weeks and months and maybe years
      and you realise it's love
          you'd just forgotten what it felt like

and you are ready to be loved again
and you are ready to be wonderful again
and you are ready to be vulnerable and terrified and scared
you are ready to make mistakes and have your heart broken
and start again

      because the odds don't have to be that against you
      it doesn't have to be life or death
      violence or survival
      every time

your abuser set those terms
it's time you set your own

      and it's like the first snow
      and it's like the cherry blossoms blooming
      and it's like unravelling and unspooling

having no idea where it will end
only that you'll follow her anywhere
that smile and those eyes
and that way of making you feel
      like you've got everything to gain
        and her hand in yours
            is where it starts

           again

the force

she tells me
the force of the two of us together
                                        is so strong

                          that if we need to get out of bed
                    for water or work
            what the hell
we might as well change the world
                                        while we're at it

            piece of cake
            she says

                    so we stay between the sheets
                savour the might of us
        when we don't have to fight
against anything

except time

too in love to protest

late-night drunk on kisses and hope
we plan out paths forward
                    where we don't need to get up tomorrow

'what do you want?' I ask her
'fully automated luxury queer spaceship socialism!' she answers
        I smile
                kiss her
                        forget to set the alarm

        we've fallen too in love
        to get up in time to protest

                    instead we stay in bed
            tracing revolutions like constellations on each other's skin
watching the sun pass us by outside the window

like children
we have so much patience with each other
                        and so little with the world

we use love as healing
as method and meaning
as if it could change it all   but, honey, it can't

                            no matter how queer
                    our loving is not revolution
        we cannot let ourselves off the hook
quite this easily

it is not enough
to kiss away the pain
            the root of the pain itself
                    must be amended

        so let's get out of bed, darling
        let's step out onto the barricades
                our care cannot end with one another
                no matter how convenient that would be

it will always be easier
to love you
than to build a world
where we don't have to work so hard
to love ourselves

love and revolution

we fell into love and friendship
    over revolutionary theory
    and large mugs of tea
    at demonstrations and strikes
        over the exhausted bags beneath our eyes

    our relationships
        were always based on the willingness to say
        'I know the world is heavy to carry
        but you don't need to do it on your own'

        we learnt to be dependent on each other
    to remind one another
it is OK if all you did today
was get out of bed

to see the world in all its horror
is to never be able to look away
    ignorance is comfortable
        paying attention
        is painful but necessary
            if anything is to change

there
at the cross-section
is where our love was made
our bonds were built
our lives rested

in the knowledge
    that there is a bigger fight ahead
        but we can hold each other while we fight it

what can't we face if we're together?

on days when everything seems impossible

my friends send me dragon emojis and rainbow flags
pictures of their pets saying *YOU CAN DO IT!*
old country songs about how I'm too perfect to be humble

      I laugh
      and get on with making things possible

           nothing I have ever done
           I could have done without you

                without there being an us
                to return to

silver lining

thank you
for reminding me

      I am capable
      of being an idiot in love

            I already knew
            I could be an idiot

                  and this is a pretty great
                  silver lining

we revolt anyway

'If you are free, you need to free somebody else. If you have some power, then your job is to empower somebody else.'

Toni Morrison

resilience

the refusal to give up

despite all the evidence

yet to do

it's as much in the days we celebrate
as in the days we mourn

we're allowed to feel the weight
of constant movement

the growing pains
of always marching
always learning
always doing our best
to make the world
the best we think it can be

we are not perfect
not infallible
not without needs and doubts
and challenges of our own

it is not a failure to be disappointed
that we still have to protest this shit

there is nothing wrong
with being frustrated
we are not nearly there yet

but we do have to celebrate too
we do have to take inventory
of all the work we've done
all the battles we've won
to give us the strength
to continue on

to do

all the growing
all the learning
all the revolting

we have yet to do

sunshine

every victory
for people over profit
and hope over hate

      has been won by people
                  just like us

                 who had no idea
            if they could do it

      but the gut feeling
      they had to

           try

a story about a part of all our lives

(because almost all of us have burnt out)

she held herself so tightly
like her hands were a corset around her neck
    like her plans were a guillotine
    hanging over her schedule

    'make one wrong move and I'll—'

she pushed herself so hard
    became hollowed out
like bird bones made wishbones made wishes never come true
    like promises no one ever intends to keep to you

    'you're just not the kind of girl that—'

she carried the world on her shoulders
    no one had asked her to, they said
    but they also weren't helping to take the weight off
    looked perfectly content for people like her to do it all

    'responsibility and freedom go hand in hand—'

she crumbled underneath it
the pressure of the future pushing at her from every angle
    her activism became ruins caving in on themselves
        ribs imploding to reveal a worn-out heart

    'shouldn't have worn your heart on your sleeve'
    they said

    'if you hadn't tried so hard, you wouldn't be
    disappointed now'
    they said

what they meant was

if you'd never wished for a better world

you wouldn't be so exhausted

trying to live in this one

the thing called hope

we have
to believe
in better

revolt

because we have to
because we know
what we do
is never enough
to change everything

      but that to do something
      however small
      however flawed
      is always better
      than to do nothing

            because to do something
            is to remind ourselves
            that the way things are
            is not the way things have to be

      that if anyone can change things

it's all of us

enough

some days
    I feel like nothing I do
        will ever be enough

that my arms
    will always be too short
        to hold all the people in my life
            that need holding

that my legs
    will always be too weak
        to take all the stands
            that need taking

that my voice
    will always be too small
        to break all the silences
            overpower all the violences
                that echo around us

that there will never
be enough hours in the day
    to do all the political/care work
        that needs doing

        that the fact that changing the world
        is a labour of love
    means it will always feel
    exhausting
that what we do will never be enough

but then I do what I can

I use the time I have
    I march / I speak / I sing / I hug someone
        I care for something more than myself

and recognise
that this is what gives me hope
this is what gives me strength

this is what gives me resilience

that if this is all I can do
today
then it has to be
enough

because it will help others
do more
tomorrow

this

this is it
the sign you've been waiting for

      I know you've been doubting
          treading lightly
              worried how it'll all turn out

          but if you still want to do it
      if you know in your heart
it's what you have to do

this is it
the sign you've been waiting for

go, try, start

affirmations

we need to resist
I tell my reflection
toothbrush in mouth
the aftertaste of coffee and the morning paper
still sloshing around my stomach

> *we need to resist*
> I tell the bathroom mirror
> the hollow eyes staring back at me
> without answers

> this is my morning pep talk
> > not *you are beautiful*
> > not *you are brilliant*
> > not *even you are enough*

> just this
> the recognition that nothing else matters
> unless we do this
> unless we resist

unless we meet our own eyes in the mirror
and then go out to meet other pairs
see the unslept look of them
the nightmares still nestling in memories
after the morning's news scroll

the reminder that this mirror holds only my eyes
> but in all the mirrors?
> everywhere?
> right now?
the reminder that together we form a whole
I imagine my tooth-brushing face
next to all the other faces

imagine us stood
> shoulder to shoulder
> > mirror to mirror
> > > each of us saying it

111

                              like a choir

                echoing in half-empty tiled rooms
          everywhere
    at once

we need to resist

            call it love or fury or refusal to buckle under
            call it daring to believe you are not alone

call it your morning pep talk

          and tonight
          when you look in the mirror
          toothbrush in hand
          eyes locking in on themselves

          say it like you mean it
              say it because you know it to be true
                  say it and know there is a choir of voices
                      waiting to hear it
                          coming from you

we need to resist

say it like
a promise
a prayer
a political fact
          there is no alternative to

              say it like a compass needle
              like an engine starting
              like the first voice in the choir
              the first step on the march

we need to resist

              now spit

          rinse
              repeat

the changing climate

resilience
for the rich

or

revolt
for the rest

close

I need to feel close
to you

the soft skin at the nape of your neck
the noise you make before you laugh
the way you smile in your sleep

I need to feel close
if not to you
then to me

that dawning realisation
I am holding myself
keeping myself alive and going
feeling grateful for my own company

I need to feel close
if not to one of us
then to something bigger

something like hope or change
community or revolution
something like everything that matters

something like the way distant stars
gather into galaxies
without them knowing it

the way every planet in the Milky Way
thought it was alone

until it saw

the bigger

picture

revolution

it didn't start
with laws
or governments
     and it won't end there

    it didn't start
    with meetings
    and demonstrations
       and that's not what this is for

      it started with us
      hand in hand
      arm in arm
         support in solidarity

        it started with us
     believing
   things could be
different

when they write the history books

someday
when I am old and grey
I want to remember right now
          with pride

when they write the history books
    I want to say
        'that right there
            those were the change-makers and I'

    the future frightens me
    some days it feels
    as if we've already
    lost

      I want us
      to remind ourselves
      every day
    that we have not

         the fight isn't over yet
         there is still a path ahead
         and we follow in the footsteps
         of giants

          have inherited
        strategies and fighting spirits
      from all the demonstrations
    that came before us

their promise
    their proof

that only groups of dedicated people
have ever changed the world

so why not us?

why not this world

why not this time

why not everything

we can still make happen

how we'll build it

we're not angry
    not really
        we're exhausted
            all cried out
                done with this shit

                we're ready to tear everything down
        and build anew

it's not difficult
not really

        it's been done before
            more than often

        all it takes is enough of us
            to go out
                and start
                    building

it's getting
    so close

so come
    come bring your hands

    come bring your hands that know how to care
    how to carry someone with nothing but your heart
    as muscle strength

come
come bring your mouths
come bring your mouths that say the names of all the lives lost
to violence in the past year
your mouths that whisper promises
                kiss goodbyes
                  sing sorrows

come
come bring your eyes
come bring your eyes that see
that see all the world's misery
that are tear-gassed and crying
       that are galaxies birthed and dying
          with every instance of oppression

it will happen
so soon

so come
come bring your hands that hold
    that change nappies put on plasters
      try to care for those falling apart
        try to not pull people further apart

come bring your feet
come bring your boots your tired toes your bare heels
    run to the place where we meet
      you know where it is
        in the middle of it all
          beneath the earth's surface

    come look each other in the eyes
    come believe in something better
    if you know that something's gotta change
    that anything less is   impossible

come meet each other's gaze
come hear each other's words
come decide
together
that

this
is
when it happens

    and they come running
    dancing jumping skipping in confetti cavalcades

and they hold each other's hands
carry hug uplift one another

and they speak with one tongue
shout kiss whisper promise the answers

and the demonstration is not going forwards
it does not end in front of a building or town square

it continues upwards
into the air
and keeps
rising

and
it does not stop happening

and they dance their way
upwards together
inwards together

and they build something
that has never been seen before

songs that are made
only when they are sung

promises that become truth
the second they are spoken

steps that become real
as soon as a foot searches for them

and they build it together
that which can only be built together

they build a haven a care construct
an air castle of flesh and blood

through
the hands that carry us
the mouths that kiss us
the ears that hear us
the feet that dance us
the eyes that see us

that's how we build it

the future

hope is a resource

hope is
a revolt
a resistance
a renewable resource

  when they want us to cower in corners
   and shut down with fear

    hope is a resource
      so don't you forget it

   don't you squander it
  don't you keep it to yourself
and leave it there

  like a guilty pleasure
  like a stuffed animal you've got too old for
  like the love letters you wrote as a teenager

  like that bleeding heart of yours

hope is a resource
it should be
treasured
precious
prized

because it germinates in community
  replenishes and renews its own reserves
   grows like weeds when unwatched
  hope
hope
hope!

  whisper it into pillows
  mumble it in lovers' ears

   shout it on street corners
   press it into strangers' palms
   hug it into loved ones' hearts

gather it up like dandelion fuzz
like a universe of stars
like little seeds of resistance
in your open hands
puff up your cheeks
and blow it into the wind

scatter it like confetti
spread it like sunshine
pushing through the water's surface

take a deep breath and fill your lungs with it
feel it spread on your tongue and down your throat
making it easier to breathe

feel it rollercoaster through your insides
ride shotgun with your pulse
your blood delivering it
like a mailman handing out only good news

hear your heart beating belting bettering
each repeated rhythm reminding you
another world is possible
another world is possible
another world is possible

notice the way it tingles in you
all that hope buzzing
the way it hums a melody
that keeps the threats and fears
from getting too close

smell the dandelion seeds
see how they travel with the wind right
there

hear your heartbeat

reminding you

another world

starts here

bonus: writing revolts

'You have to form communities of joy and resistance.'

Idil Eser

writing revolts: exercises in hope

To be able to keep working for a better world on days when things feel hard and hopeless, we need to be able to imagine a better world. One worth fighting for.

We need to envision that world and relate it to concrete steps that we can take every day, to make the world we live in more and more like the one we dream, hope, yearn and fight for.

Just like athletes imagining a win or someone preparing to give birth, it's not enough to be able to envision what things will look like when they go well. We need to be able to imagine what the world we're yearning for will sound like, smell like, taste like, feel like in our bodies and for the people we love.

The more of our available senses we include in our idea of a better world, the more visceral it will feel. And the more visceral it feels, the more motivating it is to start doing the work of making it real.

These exercises include five senses, but you work with as many as you feel able and comfortable with.

Finally, we need to learn to talk about the better world we imagine – with others. People like and unlike us. We need to be willing to learn from and with them. To imagine and then actively take steps together to make that world a reality.

These writing exercises are for anyone who wants to start building hope and change, regardless of whether you've written poetry before and whether or not you've engaged in some form of activism before. The only important thing is that you dare try.

These exercises are examples of tools we can use to build communities of joy and resistance together.

They are not about writing well, but joyfully revolting.

sight: envisioning better

NEED:

- a printed newspaper and a pair of scissors, OR an online article and an open file to copy and paste into

- a bit of hope

1) Take an article about how the world is going to shit.

2) Cut out only the words you need to tell a different story: one of hope instead of hate, or how things can change for the better instead of for the worse. Maybe cut out or copy an image or two, if you find ones that inspire you.

3) Rearrange your cut-out words and images to tell a new story. One of hope, or anger, or change.

4) You just wrote a cut-out poem!

And maybe built a bit of hope too.

Hope is a precious resource.

Well done you.

hearing: the revolution will not be televised

NEED:

- something to write on
- something to write with
- an internet connection
- a timer

1) Find an online audio or video recording from a recent protest or political rally whose aims you agree with.

2) Write down five sounds you can hear in the recording. You can write a word or a sentence to describe each sound. When you're done, turn off the recording.

3) Set a timer to four minutes. Using the five sounds you've written down, write a poem. Start each sentence with 'the revolt will sound like...' and finish the sentence however you like. From when the timer starts to when the timer stops, just keep writing.

4) When the timer goes off, stop writing.

You just wrote a visceral, sounds-based description of the revolt. Imagining change makes it easier to commit to. Maybe, at the next protest for this issue, you'll be right in the crowd making sounds of your own.

taste: your recipe for hope

What do you need to build hope? Resilience? The ability to keep going when the world is heading in the wrong direction?

And what about when it's not you? What do you do when someone close to you is having a hard time?

How can you create hope and nurturing the way you cook up your favourite meal?

NEED:

- something to write on
- something to write with
- a timer

1) List three ingredients included in one of your favourite comfort meals.

2) List three things you do to help yourself or a loved one feel better when things feel hopeless. Is there someone you talk to? Something you do for or with someone? Someplace you go together?

3) You now have your ingredients and activities listed. Set a timer to four minutes and write a recipe for what you need to do when things feel hopeless. Mix activities from (2) and ingredients from (1) and create a brand-new mash-up recipe for hope.

4) You've got your instructions – now use 'em. Next time you or a loved one are struggling, try to follow your own recipe. And if all else fails – cook your favourite comfort food.

smell: a whiff of the good life

Smells are closely related to memories and emotions, sometimes bringing up things we've entirely forgotten until we catch a whiff of them, like a long-forgotten feeling.

Let's use the power of smells (or, if you, like me, have a near-nonexistent sense of smell, the even-larger power of your imagination) to put into words what a good life feels like.

NEED:

- something to write on

- something to write with

- a timer

1)   Write down three smells you associate with a good life. For me, it's the scent of books in my favourite library, the smell of hot cocoa, and taking a deep breath of pine tree air in the forest near my mother's house.

2)   Write down three smells you associate with care and community. Mine would be the smell of butternut soup cooking, of my bedsheets against my cheek, and of coffee brewing in a large pot at a political meeting.

3)   Write down three smells you associate with hope. For me, it'd be the smell of the first spring flowers, of tea at the café where my best friend and I meet up, and the smell of the first snow falling.

4)   Take your nine written-down smells and, using these, write a poem about what a good life is for you. Set a timer to four minutes, and write without stopping.

5)   When the timer goes off, stop writing.

Now that you've mapped out what a good life means for you, don't hesitate to prioritise the people, places and activities that you associate with goodness, care, community and hope.

The more you build your own capacity to celebrate the good and cope with the bad, the more you are able to make a continued positive change in the world.

Living a good life can be part of making a better world.

touch: what change feels like

NEED

- something to write on

- something to write with

- a timer

- a memory

1) Think of a time when you felt part of making the world a better place. Or felt in your bones that things were changing for the better. Or witnessed for yourself how kind and caring people can be. What was it like? What happened? How did it feel?

2) Set a timer to five minutes. Write a poem about this memory, focusing on what it felt like at the time – in your body, on your skin, within your feelings. Make it as visceral and bodily as possible. Did your heart speed up? Did you smile until your face muscles ached? Was the wind hot or cold? Did you hold someone's hand? Don't judge what you write. Just keep writing.

3) When the timer goes off, stop writing.

Next time you need a reminder of what it is we're fighting for when we're fighting for a better world, read this poem to yourself. Think about this memory. And next time things feel this good because of a change or improvement you are part of, don't forget to celebrate it and take a moment to take it all in.

This is fuel for future fights.

bonus writing exercise: creating in community

You need to be at least two people for this exercise, but can be as many as you want. You do not need to be in the same physical place, and could do it over the phone or the internet.

NEED

- something to write on

- something to write with

- friends, neighbours, family members, strangers or loved ones to do this exercise with

1) Set a timer to three minutes.

2) Write a poem where every sentence starts with 'I want to live in a world where…'

3) Find a person or a group of people to do the exercise with you – young or old, close or distant, experienced poetry writers or total newcomers, convinced activists or complete beginners.

4) When you've all done the exercise, add your poems together, mixing lines from their poem(s) and yours, writing a new collective poem together. Feel free to add new lines together, or to repeat a line you like especially. If you want, change the wording to 'we want to live in a world where…'

5) You have now written your very own collective manifesto. Talk about how you might make that kind of world come about, and how you can help, together and each of you individually, in making it real.

outro: how we revolt every day

Nurturing and nourishing, building communities, caring and creating, loving and learning, and revolting anyway – these are things we must do in order to keep going. In order to build hope and collective resistance.

When done consciously, and actively, they are part of bringing about a better world.

When done in the context of actively trying to create political change, they are not only joyful and meaningful, but damn effective.

When done hand-in-hand with working for racial and LGBTQIA+ justice, for gender equality and trans rights, for social, economic and environmental sustainability – for a future we can all believe in, live in and live for – they are daily forms of revolt.

They are how we change the world while living in it.

thank you

to all the people who help me revolt by caring for me and allowing me to care for them.

Thank you to my inherited family. The whole inosculation of you. For meals cooked and bandages changed. For love and laughter. For unending support.

Thank you to my chosen queer family. To lifelong bestie Agnes for each reminder that our lives and loves are revolutions of their own. To my incredible friends. To my housemates for feeding me tea and making me go outside to catch the sunshine. To my nerdy friends for distracting me from overworking with dragons and magic.

Thank you to my writing community. To my writer wife, Emily, who keeps me writing and laughing and reminds me what matters, time and again. None of this would have been possible without you.

Thank you to all the people who keep me creating for the pure joy of it. To the New Guard (Det Nya Gardet), my feminist spoken word collective who have made me believe, again, that writing can be revolutionary and still feel good to do. Every day. Saga, Josefin, Hanna, I didn't know truly know what writing and touring were until I wrote and toured with you.

To my coursemates and teachers in studying the work of Audre Lorde and writing together. Believing, truly, that our silences will not protect us. That we must break them together.

Thank you to my publisher Burning Eye. For having my back and daring to be political. To Bridget for touring support and lifesaving friendship. To Clive for believing in this book before I did.

Thank you to everyone who has booked me for gigs, gone to my workshops, bought my books, supported my crowdfunded spoken word videos. Thank you for helping me pay rent and buy food while I wrote this book and all the books to come.

Because of course there will be more books.

Finally, thank you to every activist and every movement for social justice that proves, time and again, that things can change.

For all the tireless work you do to make this planet a better place.

I believe, and I hope you do too, that our best and most revolutionary days are still ahead of us.

Agnes Török
Stockholm, 9 September 2019

space to write:

space to write:

space to write:

space to write:

space to write:

space to write:

space to write:

space to write:

space to write:

space to write:

space to write:

space to write:

space to write:

space to write:

Lightning Source UK Ltd.
Milton Keynes UK
UKHW050750310320
361079UK00006B/23

9 781911 570714